LA ROSE

LA ROSE

AN INTIMACY OF ROSES

TRUE REDD

WESTERN EYE PRESS

TELLURIDE

LA ROSE
AN INTIMACY OF ROSES
is published by
Western Eye Press
Box 917, Telluride
Colorado 81435

All photographs
© 1990 True Redd

Sources for the quotations that
accompany the photographs
are given on pages 96 & 97,
along with copyright data
& acknowledgement
of permission to reprint,
where applicable.

ISBN 0-941283-07-0 softbound
ISBN 0-941283-08-9 hardbound

The text of LA ROSE
is set in a modern
version of Garamond,
a type first designed
in the 16th century
by Claude Garamond.
Book design by
True Redd &
Lito Tejada-Flores.
Production coordination
by Joanne Bolton

Printed in Korea
by Sung In Printing Co. Ltd.

To order copies
of the gallery-quality
poster of LA ROSE,
write to:
La Rose / Western Eye Press
Box 917, Telluride, CO 81435

to John & Marsha Evans
for their love and friendship
that goes back long before roses

Une rose seule, c'est toutes les roses

et celle-ci: l'irremplaçable,

le parfait, le souple vocable

encadré par le texte des choses.

One single rose is all roses,

and this particular one, unique,

perfect, a supple word with which to speak

the text of all things.

Rainer Maria Rilke

ῥοδοδάκτυλοσ ῾ηώσ…
rosy-fingered dawn…

Homer

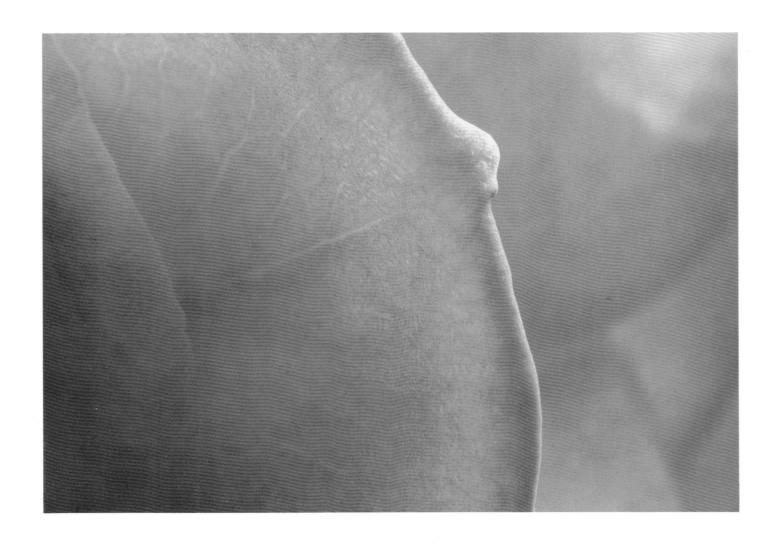

…like a rose-pink winter sunrise…

Wallace Stegner

You may break, you may shatter the vase, if you will,
but the scent of the roses will hang round it still.

Thomas Moore

Sur tout parfum j'aime la rose.
Among all perfumes, I prefer the rose.

Pierre de Ronsard

All night by rose, rose—
All night by the rose I lay;
Dared I not the rose steal,
Yet I bore the flower away.

    English folksong, 13th century

Wenn's schneiet rote Rosen,
Und regnet kühlen Wein,
So kommst du auch nicht wieder,
Herzallerliebster mein.

When it shall snow red roses,
When it shall rain cool wine,
Then thou shall't come no more,
O fullheart love of mine.

     German folksong, 15th century.

Tant de fois je t'ai vue…
dans un coffret odorant, à côté d'une mèche,
ou dans un livre aimé qu'on relira seul.

How many times have I seen you…
in a perfumed jewel box, beside a lover's lock
or in a beloved book that one rereads alone.

Rainer Maria Rilke

In einem Buch blätternd fand
Ich eine Rose welk, zerdrückt,
Und weiß auch nicht mehr, wessen Hand
Sie einst für mich gepflückt.

Leafing through a book I found,
a pressed and faded rose,
and no longer knew whose hand
had picked it for me once.

Nikolaus Lenau

And I will make thee a bed of roses
And a thousand fragrant posies...
And if these pleasures may thee move,
Come live with me and be my love

   Christopher Marlowe

From fairest creatures we desire increase
That thereby beauty's rose might never die.

William Shakespeare

Les destins sont jaloux de nos prospérités,
Et laissent plus durer les chardons que les roses.

Fate is jealous of our fortune, and choses
to let thistles outlive roses.

Honorat de Bueil

—is love a rose you can buy and give away…?

Carl Sandburg

Nel giallo de la rosa sempiterna
che si dilata, ed ingrada, e redole
odor di lode al Sole che sempre verna…

Into the yellow of the forever sun
  which expands in tiers, and grows, and spreads
  its scent of praise to the ever greening sun…

  Dante

Listen and you will hear—st . . th . . st . . th . . st . . th . .
it is the feet of the yellow roses climbing up and down
and leaning out and curving and nearly falling . .

Carl Sandburg

Rose leaves, when the rose is dead,
Are heap'd for the beloved's bed;
And so thy thoughts, when Thou art gone,
Love itself shall slumber on.

           Percy Bysshe Shelly

Sweet as the breath of roses blown
The fragrance of her life.

Alice E. Allen

Each morn a thousand Roses brings, you say;
Yes, but where leaves the Rose of Yesterday?

The Rubáiyát of Omar Khayyám

Ah, quand refleuriront les roses de septembre!
Ah, when will they bloom again, the roses of September!

Paul Verlaine

...I wish
The sky would rain down roses, as they rain
From off the shaken bush. Why will it not?
Then all the valleys would be pink and white,
And soft to tread on.

George Eliot

Unseen buds, infinite, hidden well,
Under the snow and ice, under the darkness, in every square or cubic inch,
Germinal, exquisite, in delicate lace, microscopic, unborn…

Walt Whitman

A rose is sweeter in the bud than full blown.

John Lyly

ch'i' ho vedutto tutto il verno prima
  lo prun mostrarsi rigido e feroce,
  poscia portar la rosa in su la cima;

for I have seen, stiff and sharp,
  the thornbush stand all winter long,
  then finally bear a rose upon its top

Dante

Then I went to my Pretty Rose tree
To tend her by day and by night;
But my Rose turned away with Jealousy,
And her thorns were my only delight.

                   William Blake

There must be a place
a room and a sanctuary
set apart for silence
for shadows and roses...

Carl Sandburg

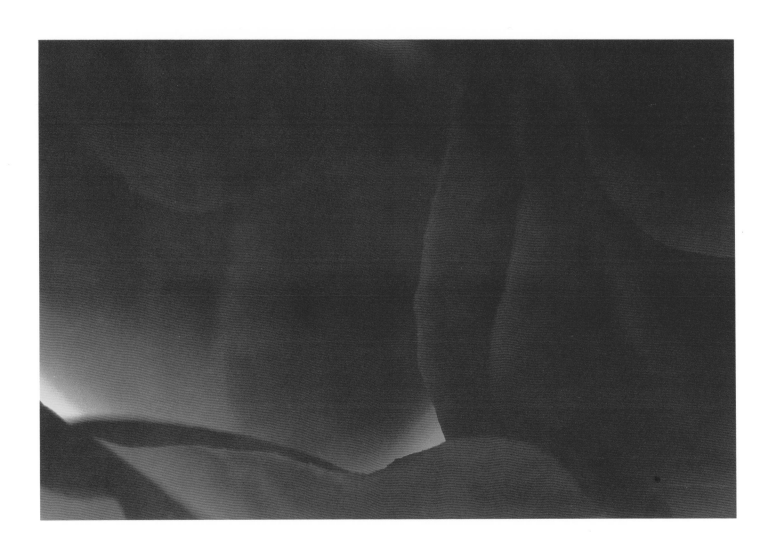

A sepal, petal and a thorn
Upon a common summer's morn
A flask of Dew–a Bee or two–
A Breeze–a caper in the trees–
And I'm a Rose!

      Emily Dickinson

Yo persigo una forma que no encuentra mi estilo,
boton de pensamiento que busca ser la rosa.

I am pursuing a form that my style does not find,
a bud of thought which seeks to become a rose.

Rubén Darío

Die Ros' ist ohn' warum,
sie blühet weil sie blühet,

The rose has no reason why,
She blooms because she blooms,

Angelus Silesius

What's in a name? That which we call a rose,
by any other name would smell as sweet.

William Shakespeare

The wilderness and the solitary place shall be glad for them; and the desert shall rejoice, and blossom as the rose.

Isaiah 35:1

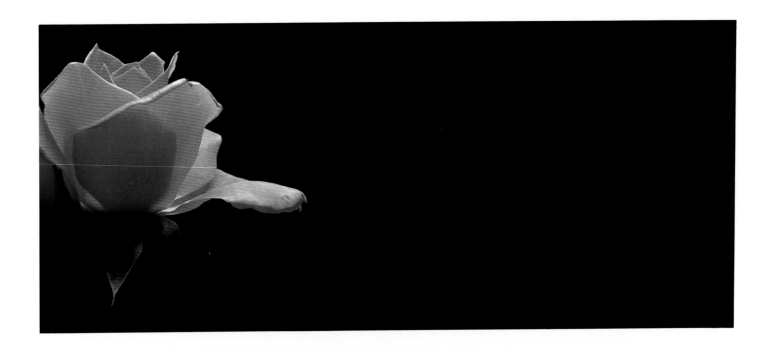

The Rose doth deserve the chiefest and most principall place among all floures whatsover...

Great Herball of 1560

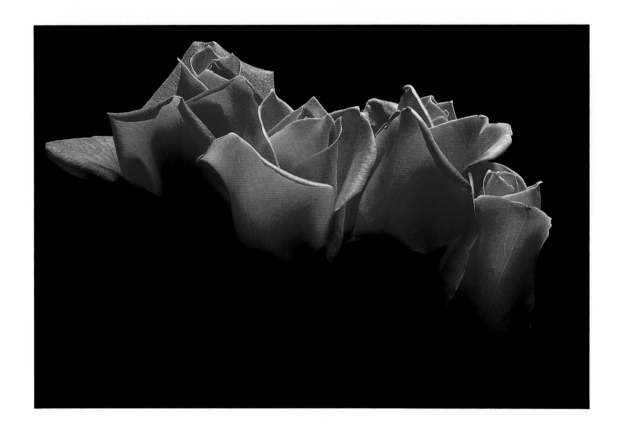

"I haven't much time to be fond of anything....But when I have a moment's fondness to bestow, most times…the roses get it."

Wilkie Collins

There's a yellow rose in Texas
I'm going there to see,
No other fellow knows her,
not half so well as me.

American folksong, 19th century

And I don't want no wiltin' flowers on my grave;
Cowboy, all I want's just one red rose.

                                    Ernie Fanning

…and she was
the loveliest little being
one could imagine,
and as tender
and fair as the
most beautiful
rose-leaf.

       Hans Christian Andersen

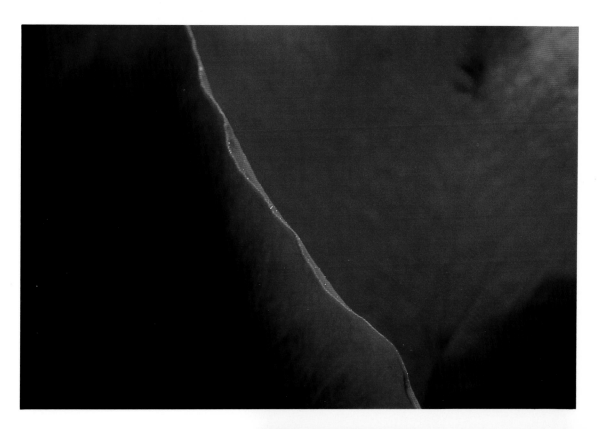

Heavy heavy is love to carry
and light as one rose petal...

Carl Sandburg

La rosa
no buscaba ni ciencia ni sombra:
confín de carne y sueño,
buscaba otra cosa.

The rose
was not searching for darkness or science:
borderline of flesh and dream,
it was searching for something else.

Federico García Lorca

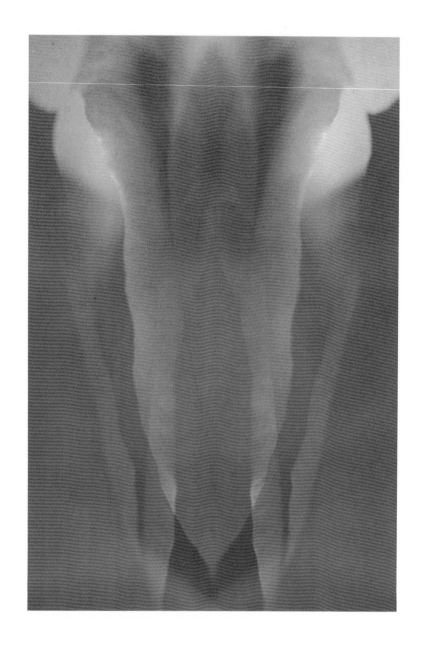

Time tracks the sound of shape on man and cloud,
On rose and icicle the ringing handprint.

Dylan Thomas

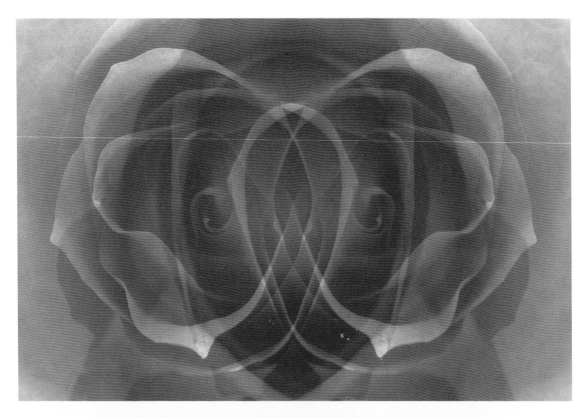

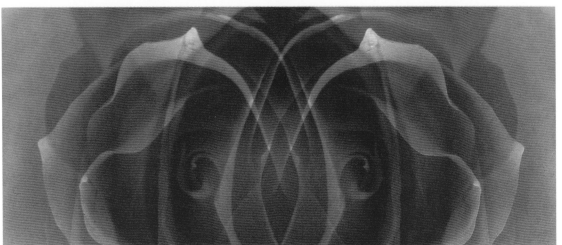

I count the days till Judgement Day.
The streets are stained with lurid fires,
bonfires of roses in the snow.

      Anna Akhmatova

She sped as Petals of a Rose
Offended by the Wind –
A frail Aristocrat of time…

Emily Dickinson

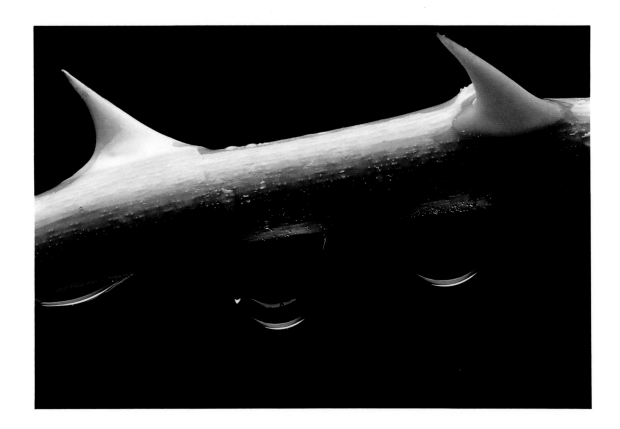

But earthlier happy is the rose distill'd
Than that which withering on the virgin thorn
Grows, lives and dies in single blessedness

William Shakespeare

Roses today, fresh roses,
fresh-cut roses today
a rose for you sir,
the ladies like roses,
now is the time,
fresh roses sir.

      Carl Sandburg

Where gat you that joup o' the lily scheen?
That bonnie snood of the birk sae green?
And these roses, the fairest that ever were seen?
Kilmeny, Kilmeny, where have you been?

James Hogg

Mignonne, allons voir si la rose
Qui ce matin avait declose
Sa robe de pourpre au soleil,
A point perdu cette vesprée
Les plis de sa robe pourprée
Et son teint au votre pareil.

Darling, go see if that rose
which of a morning shows
its purple robe to the sun,
by evening hasn't shed
its dress's folds of red,
its color so like your own.

Pierre de Ronsard

O my Luve is like a red, red rose, that's newly sprung in June;
O my Luve is like a melodie, that's sweetly played in tune!

Robert Burns

Seul, ô abondante fleur,
tu crées ton propre espace;
tu te mires dans une glace
d'odeur

Alone, extravagant bloom
you create your own space;
alone you retrace
your image in a mirror of perfume.

Rainer Maria Rilke

[Beauty is] the
omnipresence of
death and
loveliness, a
smiling sadness
that we discern
in nature and all
things, a mystic
communion that
the poet feels—
an expression
of it can be
a dustbin with
a shaft of light
across it, or
it can be a rose
in the gutter.

Charlie Chaplin

Wishing for roses, I walk through the garden
Where the world's reddest rose leans from a wall.

    Anna Akhmatova

for it is just one more flame of a rose
that came with its red blush and crimson bloom
and did the best it could with what it had…

Carl Sandburg

Was it not Fate that, on this July midnight—
Was it not Fate (whose name is also Sorrow)
That bade me pause before the garden-gate,
To breathe the incense of those slumbering roses?

Edgar Allen Poe

Die Rosen leuchten immer noch,
die dunklen Blätter zittern sacht;
ich bin im Grase aufgewacht,
o kämst du doch,
es ist so tiefe Mitternacht.

Dark leaves trembling soft,
these roses still cast light;
in the grass I woke upright,
ah, if only you would come,
this dark, this deep midnight.

Richard Dehmel

A rose or a hyacinth in bloom
can blind you.

     Dahlia Ravikovitch

…roses on fire are two times red…

Vreni Jonsdotter

They are not long, the days of wine and roses;
Out of a misty dream
Our path emerges for awhile, then closes
Within a dream.

      Ernest Dowson

And the rose herself has got
Perfume which on earth is not;

John Keats

and you can waltz and tango wearing your sweet crimson rose
and take it home and lay it on a window sill and see it…

Carl Sandburg

The things which I have seen I now can see no more!
The rainbow comes and goes,
And lovely is the rose;

William Wordsworth

Ehret die Frauen!
Sie flechten und weben
Himmlische Rosen
Ins irdische Leben.

Honor women!
They braid and they weave
Heavenly roses
Into earthly life.

Friedrich von Schiller

"Rosebud!"

Citizen Kane

"Cherchez les effets et les causes,"
Nous disent les rêveurs moroses.
Des mots! des mots! Cueillons les roses!

"Seek after effects and causes,"
gloomy philosopers tell us.
Words, just words! Gather roses!

Théodore de Banville

Vivez, si m'en croyez, n'attendez à demain.
Cueillez dès aujourd'hui les roses de la vie.

If you believe me, live! don't wait for tomorrow.
Gather this very day, the roses of life.

Pierre de Ronsard

Gather therefore the Rose, whilst yet is prime
For soon comes age, that will her pride de-flower:
Gather the rose of love, whist yet is time.

Edmund Spenser

roseheart
rosestorm
raining
roses
roseheart
rosewind
galeforce
roses
roseheart
rosequake
heartbreak
roses
roseheart
rosehands
roselips
roses

A. B. Retif

… c'est un monde qui tourne en rond
pour que son calme centre ose
le rond repos de la ronde rose.

…it is the world turning in air
that its calm center might dare
the round repose of a round rose

Rainer Maria Rilke

She didn't like the eating part when there were people that made her shy and often wondered why you couldn't eat something poetical like violets or roses....

James Joyce

The savour of the Roses swote
Me smote right to the herte rote.

                    Chaucer

I remember, I remember
The roses, red and white,
…
Those flowers made of light.

Thomas Hood

roses as pale
as dreams
of other roses
dreamed
by other roses…

        Lito Tejada-Flores

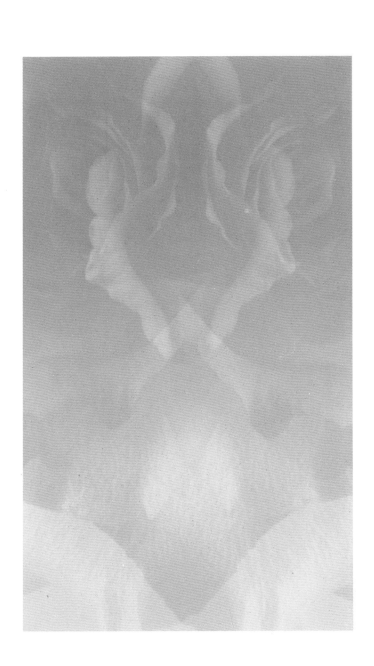

"Love is a door we shall open together."
So they told each other under the moon
One evening when the smell of leaf mould
And the beginnings of roses and potatoes
Came on a wind.

Carl Sandburg

Dich lieb' ich wie die Rose ihren Strauch…
It's you I love as the rose loves its rosebush.

Friedrich Rückert

Lost inside the labyrinth of the rose,
I look for meaning, find only beauty;
to bloom and fade is the roses duty,
but why?—it neither asks nor knows.

Edward Saavedra

The red rose whispers of passion
And the white rose breathes of love;
O, the red rose is a falcon,
And the white rose is a dove.

John Boyle O'Reilly

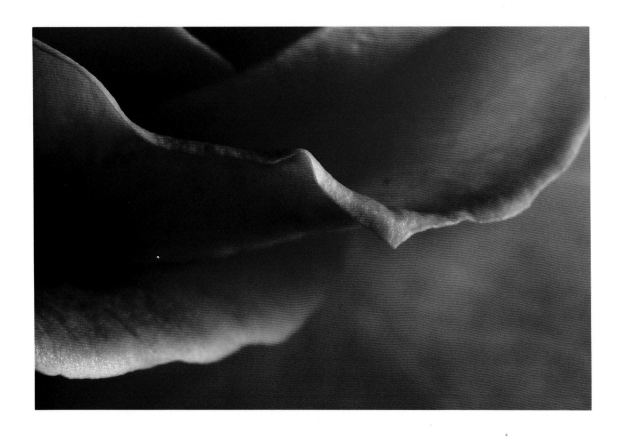

And her lips reminded people of deep red roses
waiting in the cool of the summer evening

       Carl Sandburg

Mitte sectari, rosa quo locorum sera moretur.
Cease your efforts to find where the last rose lingers.

Horace

A restfulness arises from contemplating a quiet white rose until the rose expands into the whiteness of sleep.

Truman Capote

S O U R C E S

7 "One single rose is all roses…"
   Rainer Maria Rilke (1875-1926)
   from VI in *Les Roses*, one of almost 400
   poems this German poet wrote in French,
   translated by Lito Tejada-Flores

8 "Rosy-fingered dawn…"
   Homer (c.700 B.C.)
   often-used phrase in the *Illiad* and *Odyssey*

9 "…like a rose-pink winter sunrise…"
   Wallace Stegner
   from *Angle of Repose*

10 "You may break, you may shatter…"
   Thomas Moore (1779-1852)
   from *Farewell! But Whenever*

11 "Among all perfumes, I prefer…."
   Pierre de Ronsard (1524-1585)
   from "Ode to Cassandre"

14 "How many times have I seen you…"
   Rainer Maria Rilke
   from XIII in *Les Roses*

15 "Leafing through a book I found,…"
   Nikolaus Lenau, (1802-1850)

16 "And I will make thee a bed of roses…"
   Christopher Marlowe (1564-1593)
   from *The Passionate Shepherd to His Love*

17 "From fairest creatures we desire increase…"
   William Shakespeare (1564-1616)
   from *Sonnets*, I

18 "Fate is jealous of our fortune and chooses…"
   Honrat de Bueil (1589-1670)
   from the "Sonnet to the duc de Guise."

19 "—is love a rose you can buy…?"
   Carl Sandburg (1878-1967)
   from "Little Word, Little White Bird" in
   Honey and Salt,

20 "Into the yellow of the forever rose…"
   Dante Alighieri (1265-1321)
   from *The Divine Comedy, Paradisio, C.30*

21 "Listen and you will hear…"
   Carl Sandburg
   from "How Six Pigeons Came Back to
   Hatrack the Horse After Many Accidents and
   Six Telegrams" in *Rootabaga Stories*

22 "Rose leaves, when the rose is dead…"
   Percy Bysshe Shelly (1792-1822)
   from "Music, When Soft Voices Die"

24 "Sweet as the breath of roses blown…"
   Alice E. Allen
   from "My Mother's Garden"

26 "Each morn a thousand Roses brings…"
   from *The Rubáiyát of Omar Khayyám*
   (c.1123) trans. by Edward Fitzgerald in 1879

27 "Ah, when will they bloom again…"
   Paul Verlaine (1844-1896)
   from *Sagesse*

28 "…I wish/The sky would rain down roses…."
   George Eliot (1819-1880)
   from *The Spanish Gypsy*

29 "Unseen buds, infinite, hidden well..."
Walt Whitman (1819-1892)
from "Unseen Buds" in *Goodbye My Fancy /*
Leaves of Grass

30 "A rose is sweeter in the bud..."
John Lyly (c.1554-1606)
from *Euphues and His England*

31 "for I have seen, stiff and sharp..."
Dante Alighieri
from *The Divine Comedy, Paradisio, C.13*

32 "Then I went to my Pretty Rose tree..."
William Blake (1757-1827)
from "My Pretty Rose Tree" in
Songs of Innocence and Experience

33 "There must be a place..."
Carl Sandburg
from "Alone and Not Alone"
in *Honey and Salt*

34 "A sepal, petal and a thorn..."
Emily Dickinson (1830-1886)
number 19 in *Complete Poems*

35 "I am pursuing a form..."
Rubén Darío (1897-1916)
from *Prosas Profanas y Otros Poemas*

36 "The rose has no reason why..."
Angelus Silesius
17th Century German Mystic

37 "What's in a name? That which we call..."
William Shakespeare
from *Romeo and Juliet, Act II*

39 "The wilderness and the solitary place ..."
Isaiah, 35:1,
in the *King James Bible*

40 "The rose doth deserve the chiefest..."
John Gerarde
in *The Great Herball of 1560,*

41 "I haven't much time to be fond..."
Wilkie Collins (1824-1889)
from *The Moonstone*

42 "There's a yellow rose in Texas..."
Traditional American Ballad

43 "And I don't want no wiltin' flowers..."
Ernie Fanning
from "One Red Rose" in the collection,
Cowboy Poetry, A Gathering

44 "...and she was the loveliest little being..."
Hans Christian Andersen (1805-1875)
from *Thumbelisa*

46 "Heavy heavy is love to carry..."
Carl Sandburg
from "Solo for Saturday Night Guitar"
in *Honey and Salt*

47   "The rose
was not searching for darkness or science:..."
Federico García Lorca (1898-1936)
from "Casida de la Rosa" translated by
Robert Bly

48 "Time tracks the sound of shape..."
Dylan Thomas (1914-1954)
from "Altarwise by Owl-Light" in *Collected*
Poems

51 "I count the days till Judgement Day...."
Anna Akhmatova (1888-1966)
"Tashkent Breaks into Blossom," translated by
Richard McKane and reprinted in *A Book of*
Women Poets from Antiquity to Now

52 "She sped as Petals of a Rose..."
Emily Dickinson
from number 991 in *Complete Poems*

53 "But earthlier happy is the rose distill'd..."
William Shakespeare
from *A Midsummer-Night's Dream,* Act I

54 "Roses today, fresh roses,..."
Carl Sandburg
from "Little Word, Little White Bird," in
Honey and Salt

55 "Where gat you that joup o' the lily scheen?..."
James Hogg (1770-1835)
from "Kilmeny"

56 "Darling, go see if that rose..."
Pierre de Ronsard
from "Ode to Cassandre"

58 " O my Luve is like a red, red rose..."
Robert Burns (1759-1796)
from "A Red, Red Rose" in *Johnson's Musical*
Museum

59 "Alone, extravagant bloom..."
Rainer Maria Rilke
from XV in *Les Roses*

60 "[Beauty is] the omnipresence of death and
loveliness,..."
Charlie Chaplin (1889-1977)
from *My Autobiography*

62 "Wishing for roses, I walk through the garden...
Anna Akhmatova
from "Summer Garden" translated by Stephen
Stepanchev, reprinted in *A Book of Women Poets*
from Antiquity to Now

63 "for it is just one more flame of a rose..."
Carl Sandburg
from "Little Word, Little White Bird" in
Honey and Salt

64 "Was it not Fate that..."
Edgar Allan Poe (1809-1849)
from "To Helen"

65 "Dark leaves trembling soft..."
Richard Dehmel (1863-1920)

66 "A rose or a hyacinth in bloom..."
Dahlia Ravikovitch (Israel)
from "Poem of Explanations" in *A Book of*
Women Poets from Antiquity to Now

67 "...roses on fire..."
Vreni Jonsdotter
from "After Midnight"

68 "They are not long, the days of wine & roses..."
Ernest Dowson (1867-1900)
from "Vitae Summa Brevis Spem Nos Vetat
Incohare Longam"

69 "And the rose herself has got..."
John Keats (1795-1821)
from "Ode to the Poets"

71 "and you can waltz and tango wearing your
sweet crimson rose..."
Carl Sandburg
from "Little Word, Little White Bird," in
Honey and Salt

72 "The things which I have seen..."
William Wordsworth (1770-1850)
from "Ode on Intimations of Immortality" in
Recollections of Early Childhood

73 "Honor women!...."
Friedrich von Schiller (1759-1805)
from "Dignity of Women"

74 "Rosebud!"
the enigmatic deathbed utterance from
Orson Wells' film, *Citizen Kane*

75 "Seek after effects and causes,…"
Théodore de Banville (1823-1891)
from *Les Cariatides*

76 "If you believe me, live! don't wait…."
Pierre de Ronsard
from *Sonnets pour Hélène*

77 "Gather therefore the Rose, whilst yet is
prime…
Edmund Spenser (1552-1599)
 from *The Faerie Queene*

78 "roseheart / rosestorm…"
A. B. Retif
from *streetpoems*

79 "…it is the world turning in air…"
Rainer Maria Rilke
from XXI in *Les Roses*

80 "She didn't like the eating part …"
James Joyce (1882-1941)
from *Ulysses*

81 "The savour of the Roses swote…"
Geoffery Chaucer (c.1343-1400)
from *The Canterbury Tales*

82 "I remember, I remember…"
Thomas Hood (1799-1845)
from "I Remember! I Remember!"

85 "roses as pale as dreams…"
Lito Tejada-Flores
from a manuscript collection

86 "Love is a door we shall open together."
Carl Sandburg
 from "Moon Rondeau" in *Honey and Salt*

87 "It's you I love as the rose loves its rosebush…"
Friedrich Rückert (1788-1866, Germany)

89 "Lost inside the labyrinth of the rose…"
Edward Saavedra
from *Unpublished Poems*

90 "The red rose whispers of passion…"
John Boyle O'Reilly (1844-1890)
from "A White Rose"

92 "And her lips reminded people…"
Carl Sandburg
from "How Deep Red Roses Goes Back and
Forth Between the Clock and the Looking
Glass" in *Rootabaga Stories*

93 "Cease your efforts to find where the last rose
lingers."
Horace (Quintus Horatius Flaccus, 65-8 B.C.)
from *Odes, xxxviii*

95 "A restfulness arises from contemplating …"
Truman Capote (1924-1984)
from "White Rose" in *Dogs Bark*

A C K N O W L E D G E M E N T S

The editors wish to acknowledge and thank the following for permission to include the selections listed below:

Excerpt from *Angle of Repose* by Wallace Stegner, copyright © 1971 by Wallace Stegner. Used by permission of Doubleday, a division of Bantam, Doubleday, Dell Publishing Group, Inc.

Excerpts from *A Book of Women Poets from Antiquity to Now,* edited by Aliki Barnstone and Willis Barnstone, copyright © 1980, published by Pantheon Books,a division of Random House: Anna Akhmatova "Summer Garden" translated by Stephen Stepanachev and "Tashkent Breaks into Blossom" translated by Richard McKane; Dahlia Ravikovich "Poem of Explanations" translated by Chana Bloch; reprinted by permission of the publisher.

Excerpts from *Rootabaga Stories* by Carl Sandburg, copyright 1923 © by Harcourt Brace Jovanovich, Inc. and renewed 1951 by Carl Sandburg, reprinted by permission of the publisher.

Excerpts from *Honey and Salt*, "Moon Rondeau" and "Solo for Saturday Night Guitar" copyright ©1958 by Carl Sandburg and renewed in 1986 by Margaret Sandburg, Janet Sandburg and Helga Sandburg Crile; "Little Word, Little White Bird" copyright © 1961 by Carl Sandburg; "Alone and Not Alone" copyright © 1963 by Carl Sandburg, all reprinted by permission of Harcourt Brace Jovanovich, Inc.

Excerpt from "One Red Rose" by Ernie Fanning from *Cowboy Poetry; A Gathering* copyright © 1985 by Gibbs Smith Inc. reprinted by permission of the publisher.

Excerpt from "Casida de la Rosa" from *Lorca and Jimenez; Selected Poems* translated by Robert Bly, Beacon Press, copyright © 1973 by Robert Bly, reprinted by permission of the translator.

Excerpt from "Altarwise by Owl-Light" from *The Collected Poems of Dylan Thomas,* copyright © 1939 by New Directions Publishing Corporation, reprinted by permission of the publisher.

Excerpt from *My Autobiography* by Charlie Chaplin, copyright © 1963 by Charlie Chaplin, reprinted by permission of The Bodley Head, Ltd., London.

Excerpt from *Ulysses* by James Joyce copyright © 1934, renewed 1962 by Lucia and George Joyce, reprinted by permission of Random House, Inc.

Excerpt from "White Roses" in *Dogs Bark ; Public People in Private Places* by Truman Capote copyright © 1978 by Truman Capote, reprinted by permission of Random House, Inc.

Every effort has been made to locate copyright owners. Any not cited here will, upon notification of the publisher, be gladly acknowledged in the next printing.